SCHOLASTIC

Fill-in-the-Blank Stories

SIGHT WORDS

50 Cloze-Format Practice Pages
That Target and Teach the Top 100 Sight Words

by Linda B. Ross

New York • Toronto • London • Auckland • Sydney
Mexico City • New Delhi • Hong Kong • Buenos Aires

Teaching
Resources

Editor: Joan Novelli
Cover design by Jason Robinson
Interior design by Holly Grundon
Cover illustrations by Bari Weissman
Interior illustrations by Shelley Dieterichs

ISBN-13: 978-0-439-55431-2
ISBN-10: 0-439-55431-4
Copyright © 2008 by Linda B. Ross
All rights reserved.
Printed in the U.S.A.

1 2 3 4 5 6 7 8 9 10 40 15 14 13 12 11 10 09 08

Contents

Introduction

This book features 50 engaging cloze-format stories that provide the repeated practice children need to master 100 sight words. For each story, children use a word bank along with text and picture clues to fill in missing words. Each story offers opportunities for reading sight words in context, letting young readers practice their growing knowledge in meaningful ways, while improving fluency and comprehension. A word search provides further practice in reading and spelling all target words.

What the Research Says

Sight word knowledge is necessary for reading fluency and comprehension. As children learn to recognize sight words with accuracy and automaticity, they read more smoothly and at a faster rate. The sight words for the stories in this book were selected from the Dolch Basic Sight Vocabulary. Generated by E. W. Dolch in 1941, this list is comprised of 220 words (no nouns), which account for more than 50 percent of the words primary-age children encounter most frequently in the print materials they use. (Johns, 1976; as cited in *Phonics From A to Z* by Wiley Blevins; Scholastic, 2006)

What's Inside?

From Bear and his friends to a busy monkey named Marty, the characters in these charming stories will bring children back again and again to build essential reading skills. Each student page follows a format that children will quickly learn to recognize. This repetition allows them to focus their energies on learning the words rather than figuring out what to do. Here's a look at the components for each page.

Sight Words: The heading at the top of each story page identifies the target sight words. Each story provides practice with two words.

Fill-In Story: A cloze format invites children to fill in words to complete each story. Stories are carefully structured to meet the needs of early readers.

Word Bank: This list provides students with all the word choices they need to complete the story.

Illustration: An illustration accompanies each story, and supports early readers in understanding the text.

Word Search: This puzzle invites children to locate the target story words, providing additional opportunities to practice reading and spelling each word.

Teaching With the Stories

You can use the stories in any order that best supports your goals for whole-class, small-group, and individual instruction. Model for children how to complete a page before having them do so on their own.

1. Display a story page so all children can see it (for example, by using an overhead).

2. Read the directions aloud, and then direct children's attention to the Word Bank. Point to each word in order as you read it.

3. Direct children's attention to the title of the story. Read aloud the title, noticing any words that also appear in the Word Bank. You might take a moment to notice the illustration, and think aloud about what the story might be about.

4. As you read the story, model concepts of print, including where to begin, going from left to right, and the return sweep to the next line. Pause at each blank to think aloud about which word belongs in the blank. (It may be helpful for children to read on past a blank to finish a sentence, as the end of the sentence might provide clues to the missing word.) This is a good opportunity to teach strategies for figuring out the correct word choice, such as by making connections to the text. For example, in "Let's Eat!" (page 29), direct children's attention to the second sentence: "They were hungry and wanted to ___." Ask, "What do you want to do when you're hungry? What word do you think makes sense here?" Guide students to recognize that making connections to what they read can help them figure out unknown words. Write in the word, and continue. Point out that children will use each word in the Word Bank more than once.

5. When you have filled in all of the blanks, read the story, modeling characteristics of fluency, such as using appropriate expression and pausing at punctuation.

6. Complete the Word Search, showing children how to look across, down, and diagonally—but not backward—for the words in the Word Bank. Once you find each word four times, read the words aloud. (Students might use tally marks to keep track of how many times they find each word.)

Teaching Tip

After modeling how to use a story page, you might invite students to take turns at the overhead, modeling for you how to complete the same page (use a fresh copy). This will encourage independence as they complete story pages on their own.

Connections to the Language Arts Standards

Teaching Tip

The activity pages in this book also support components of the Reading First program (U.S. Department of Education): phonemic awareness, phonics, vocabulary development, reading fluency, and reading comprehension strategies.

The story pages and extension activities in this book are designed to support you in meeting the following standards as outlined by Mid-continent Research for Education and Learning (McREL), an organization that collects and synthesizes national and state curriculum standards—and proposes what teachers should provide for their students to become proficient in language arts, among other curriculum areas.

Reading

- Understands how print is organized and read
- Uses mental images based on pictures and print to aid in comprehension of text
- Uses meaning clues to aid comprehension and make predictions
- Uses phonetic and structural analysis to decode unknown words
- Understands level-appropriate sight words and vocabulary
- Knows main ideas or theme, setting, main characters, main events, sequence, and problems in stories
- Summarizes information found in texts (retells in own words)
- Makes simple inferences regarding the order of events and possible outcomes
- Relates stories to personal experiences

Source: *Content Knowledge: A Compendium of Standards and Benchmarks for K–12 Education* (4th ed.). Mid-continent Research for Education and Learning, 2004.

Classroom Management Tips

Whether you photocopy each story page at the time of use, or prepare class sets of the stories in advance, a simple storage system will make it easy to build a collection that you can keep on hand for later use or repeated practice.

- Place each set of stories in a file folder. Tape or glue a sample page to the front for reference, or label the tab with the sight words and title.
- To encourage self-checking, create an answer key, filling in the words to each story and circling the words in the word search. Attach to the back of the envelope or file folder. Or, place answer keys in a binder. (For a complete set of answers, see pages 10–14.)

Activities to Use With Any Story

The activities here are designed to extend what students learn with the story pages. Use them to provide additional practice with sight word recognition, to improve fluency and comprehension, and as springboards for students' own writing.

Sight Words Mini-Lesson

Use this mini-lesson as a model to provide explicit instruction for the sight words featured in each story.

1. Use each word in a sentence, and write it on a whiteboard or on chart paper. Underline the sight words.

2. Notice with children special features of words in the stories—for example, point out that the words *you* and *your* from "What Did You Forget? (page 64) are almost exactly the same. *Your* is like *you*, except for the *r* on the end.

3. Point to each letter as children spell the words.

4. Invite children to trace the letters on their desks, in the air, or on a partner's back.

5. Have children write the words in a sight words notebook. Encourage children to share the notebook with their family and practice their words.

6. Add the words to a chart or word wall of sight words from the stories. Revisit the words often to read and spell them.

Word Wall Builders

Extend learning by creating word walls or charts based on featured sight words.

1. Copy target words from a story on large index cards. Use removable adhesive to create a portable word wall that children can take to their desk and then return to the wall when finished.

2. Read the words with children. Let them spell the words as you point to each letter.

3. Play word wall games to reinforce word recognition and spelling. For example, play a game of Big Word, Little Word. Say, "I'm thinking of a word that has the little word *so* in it. What is it?" (*soon*) or "I'm thinking of a word that has the little word *hen* in it. What is it?" (*when*)

Pocket Chart Practice

The short stories in this book lend themselves well to pocket chart activities. Suggestions for creating these activities follow.

Who Has the Word? Write each line of a story on a sentence strip, leaving spaces for the target words as indicated. Cut sentence strips to fit the spaces and write a sight word on each. Distribute the word cards to different children. In the pocket chart, place sentence strips in order. Read aloud the story. When you come to a missing word ask, "Who has the word that goes here?" Have children take turns placing the words in the correct spaces. (Some children will have the same word. Explain that they will all have a chance to use their word cards to complete a sentence.) Continue in this way to complete the story, and then read it aloud together.

Scrambled Stories: Write each sentence of a story on a sentence strip, filling in any missing words. Mix up the strips and place them in a pocket chart. Invite children to help you sequence the sentences to unscramble the story. Number the backs of the sentence strips so children can work independently to place the sentences in order, and then check their work. As a variation, cut apart sentences into individual words. Challenge children to arrange the words in order.

Story Hunt

Use any story for an interactive experience that encourages children to take a closer look at the text.

1. Copy a story on chart paper, leaving spaces for the missing words. Copy the Word Bank to the side. Have children help you fill in the missing words, and then read the story together.

2. Then invite children to take turns hunting for something in the story, using a highlighter to mark it when they find it. Children can locate rhyming words, hunt for commas, or highlight words that name people, places, and things, as well as action words. The possibilities are endless. For example, in "Lights On, Lights Off" (page 48), you might ask children to find the following:

    ⬡ a word that rhymes with *park* (*dark*)

    ⬡ two words with a double *o* (*looked, too*)

    ⬡ a word that is made up of two words (*flashlight* or *outside*)

    ⬡ a sentence that ends with "!"

Encouraging Comprehension

The stories in this book are short, but provide many opportunities to practice comprehension strategies. After children complete a story, revisit it together. Ask questions to help children explore their understanding of the story. For example, after reading "Her Special Day" (page 38), ask:

- Who is this story about? (*Mimi*)

- What is the first thing Mimi does after she gets out of bed? (*brushes her teeth*)

- Why do you think Mimi runs to the kitchen? (Possible answer: *She's excited about going to school.*)

- What do you think is exciting for Mimi about the first day of school? (Possible answer: *She will meet new friends and learn new things.*)

Fluency Practice

The brevity of the stories makes them just right for fluency practice.

1. Copy a story on chart paper. Have children help you fill in the missing words.

2. Read the story aloud, modeling good reading behaviors for pacing, expression, punctuation, and inflection. For example, use stories with more than one character (and dialogue) to model how to use a different voice for each character. Model how question marks and exclamation points give you clues about expression.

3. Read the story together, using an echo-reading approach. You read one line, and children repeat it, echoing your pacing, phrasing, and intonation.

4. Read the story as a group, again encouraging children to follow along with pacing, phrasing, and intonation.

Story Switcheroo

Have some fun with the stories, using the characters, settings, and events to create new stories.

1. Write characters' names on slips of paper. Place them in a bag and label it "Characters." Do the same with story settings (such as "school"), events (such as "swimming"), and problems (such as "looking for a lost cat").

2. Let children take turns choosing a slip from each bag. Use the elements to tell a new story. Write it on chart paper and let children illustrate to create a new set of stories to read.

Answer Key

Page 15
A Good Meal

Answers:
An, a, an, a,
a, an, an

Word Search Answers:
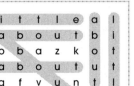

Page 20
Nice and Dry

Answers:
and, together,
and, and, and,
together, And

Word Search Answers:
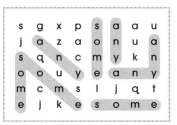

Page 16
My Little Brother

Answers:
about, about, little,
about, little, little

Word Search Answers:
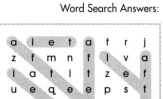

Page 21
Some Beans

Answers:
some, some, some,
any, any, some

Word Search Answers:

Page 17
Pie After Pie

Answers:
let, after, let,
let, After, let

Word Search Answers:

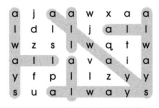

Page 22
Will It Be Sunny?

Answers:
be, be, like, like,
be, like

Word Search Answers:
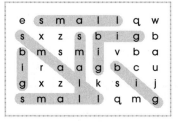

Page 18
Best of All

Answers:
always, always, all,
all, always, all

Word Search Answers:

Page 23
Big or Small?

Answers:
big, big, small,
small, small, big

Word Search Answers:

Page 19
We Are Friends

Answers:
am, are, am, am,
am, are, are

Word Search Answers:

Page 24
A Clean House

Answers:
clean, can, can, can,
clean, can, clean

Word Search Answers:
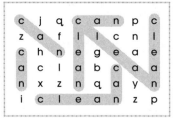

Page 25
Warm Days,
Cold Days

Answers:
warm, cold, cold,
warm, warm, cold

Word Search Answers:

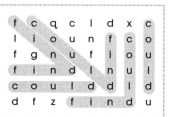

Page 30
How Fast?

Answers:
run, fast, fast, fast, run,
fast, fast, run, fast

Word Search Answers:

Page 26
How to Find Coco

Answers:
could, find, Could,
Could, could, find, find

Word Search Answers:

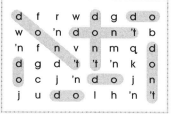

Page 31
Look for Bear

Answers:
look, for, look,
for, Look, for

Word Search Answers:

Page 27
Where Do
Animals Go?

do, don't, do,
don't, do

Word Search Answers:

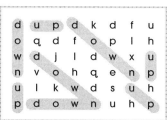

Page 32
A Funny Dream

Answers:
had, funny, had,
funny, funny, had,
funny

Word Search Answers:

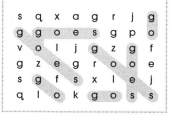

Page 28
Up and Down

Answers:
up, up, down,
down, up

Word Search Answers:

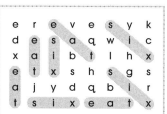

Page 33
Time to Go!

Answers:
go, goes, go, go

Word Search Answers:

Page 29
Let's Eat!

Answers:
Six, eat, six,
eat, six, eat

Word Search Answers:

Page 34
A Good Time

Answers:
my, good, my,
good, my, good

Word Search Answers:

Answer Key

Page 35
We Got Wet!

Answers:
were, were, were,
got, got, were

Word Search Answers:
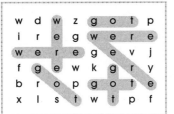

Page 36
Who Has a Riddle?

Answers:
have, has, have,
has, have

Word Search Answers:

Page 37
Is He the One?

Answers:
him, He, him,
he, He, him

Word Search Answers:
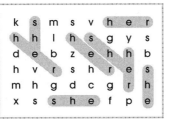

Page 38
Her Special Day

Answers:
her, she, She, her,
she, her, her

Word Search Answers:
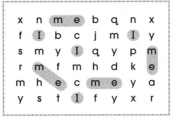

Page 39
A Present for Me

Answers:
me, I, I, I, me,
I, me, me

Word Search Answers:

Page 40
If You Move Away

Answers:
If, then, If, then,
If, then, Then

Word Search Answers:
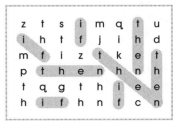

Page 41
A Long Walk

Answers:
walk, It, walk, it,
it, walk, it, it

Word Search Answers:
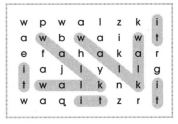

Page 42
A Big Jump!

Answers:
Our, jump, jump, our,
jump, our, Our, jump

Word Search Answers:
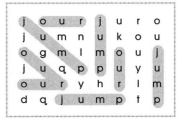

Page 43
Now I Know!

Answers:
kind, know,
kind, know

Word Search Answers:
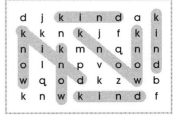

Page 44
A Long Life

Answers:
live, long, live,
live, long, live,
live, live, long

Word Search Answers:
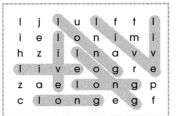

12

Answer Key

Page 45
Many Sights to See

Answers:
many, see, see, see, many, Many, see

Word Search Answers:

Page 46
An Old House

Answers:
new, old, new, old, old, new

Word Search Answers:
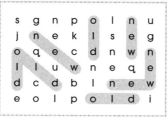

Page 47
Not Now!

Answers:
want, now, want, now, Now

Word Search Answers:
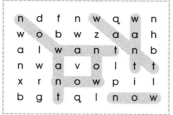

Page 48
Lights On, Lights Off

Answers:
off, on, off, on

Word Search Answers:

Page 49
Come Out and Play!

Answers:
Today, play, play, play, today

Word Search Answers:
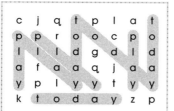

Page 50
Say "Please"

Answers:
say, please, Say, please, Please, say, please

Word Search Answers:
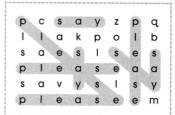

Page 51
Where Is It?

Answers:
where, put, Where, Where, put, put, where, put, where

Word Search Answers:

Page 52
I Like to Read!

Answers:
when, read, When, read, read, when

Word Search Answers:
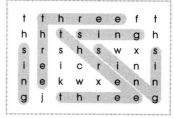

Page 53
Three Plus One

Answers:
three, sing, sing, three, sing

Word Search Answers:

Page 54
Back to Sleep

Answers:
So, sleep, sleep, so, so, sleep

Word Search Answers:
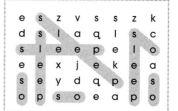

Answer Key

Page 55
Come Back Soon!

Answers:
with, with, soon,
with, soon

Word Search Answers:
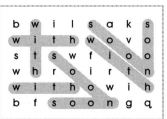

Page 60
Two Lost Chicks

Answers:
Two, too, too,
two, too

Word Search Answers:

Page 56
Thank You!

Answers:
thank, write, thank,
write, thank, write

Word Search Answers:
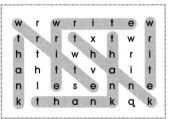

Page 61
What a Mess!

Answers:
was, What, was,
what, was, was

Word Search Answers:
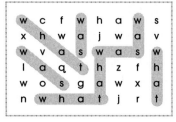

Page 57
The Best Cats

Answers:
the, them, the, them,
them, the, them

Word Search Answers:

Page 62
Up We Went!

Answers:
We, We, went, we,
We, we, We, went

Word Search Answers:
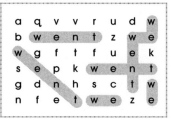

Page 58
Can They Jump?

Answers:
They, Their, They,
They, their

Word Search Answers:
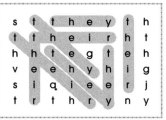

Page 63
Friends Will Help

Answers:
Who, will, will, will,
will, will, Who

Word Search Answers:
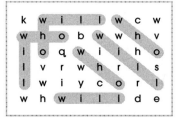

Page 59
Fun for Us!

Answers:
us, There, There,
There, us, us

Word Search Answers:
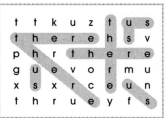

Page 64
What Did You Forget?

Answers:
you, your, your,
your, you

Word Search Answers:
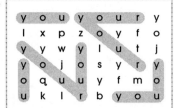

Name _____ Date _____

Look at the Word Bank.
Use the words to fill in the blanks.
Then read the story!

A Good Meal

_____ elephant went out to eat.

He looked at _____ menu.

"I'll start with _____ orange and

_____ banana," he said.

"Then I'll have _____ stack of

pancakes with _____ egg on top.

For dessert, I'll have _____ apple tart."

Word Bank

a

an

Word Search

Look at the Word Bank.
Circle the words here.
Find each word four times.
Then read the words!

a	f	s	a	v	a	k	u
h	n	l	n	j	g	y	a
d	v	i	z	e	i	h	b
j	v	u	a	z	r	c	u
m	t	g	b	a	g	j	q
x	a	n	h	w	n	c	a

Sight Words: *about, little*

Look at the Word Bank.
Use the words to fill in the blanks.
Then read the story!

Word Bank

about

little

My Little Brother

I had to write a story _____ someone

in my family.

So I wrote _____ my _____ brother.

We get along most of the time. But sometimes we

fight _____ _____ things.

Still, I love him more than a _____ bit.

In fact, I love him a lot!

Word Search

Look at the Word Bank.
Circle the words here.
Find each word four times.
Then read the words!

l	i	t	t	l	e	a	l
i	a	b	o	u	t	b	i
t	b	b	a	z	k	o	t
t	a	b	o	u	t	u	t
l	q	f	v	u	n	t	l
e	k	l	i	t	t	l	e

Sight Words: *after*, *let*

Look at the Word Bank.
Use the words to fill in the blanks.
Then read the story!

Pie After Pie

Word Bank

after

let

Duck baked some pies and _____ them cool.

Soon _____, Pig came by.

"Please _____ me have some pie," he said.

Duck _____ him have two big pieces.

_____ a while, Hen and Cat came by.

"Will you _____ us have some pie, too?"

they asked.

"That's what pies are for!" said Duck.

Word Search

Look at the Word Bank.
Circle the words here.
Find each word four times.
Then read the words!

a	l	e	t	a	f	r	j
z	f	m	n	f	l	v	a
l	a	t	l	t	z	e	f
u	e	q	e	e	p	s	t
l	e	t	y	r	x	l	e
e	q	a	f	t	e	r	r

Name _____   Date _____

Look at the Word Bank.
Use the words to fill in the blanks.
Then read the story!

Word Bank

all

always

Best of All

I'm _____ happy to see my Aunt Tina.

She _____ visits us in the spring.

I like to show her _____ of my new books.

I also like to read _____ of my poems

and stories to her.

She _____ listens very carefully.

Then she tells me which one she likes best of _____!

Look at the Word Bank.
Circle the words here.
Find each word four times.
Then read the words!

a	j	a	a	w	x	a	a
l	d	l	l	j	a	l	l
w	z	s	l	w	q	t	w
a	l	l	a	v	a	i	a
y	f	p	l	l	z	y	y
s	u	a	l	w	a	y	s

Sight Words: *am, are*

Look at the Word Bank.
Use the words to fill in the blanks.
Then read the story!

Word Bank
am
are

We Are Friends

I _____ going to a new school today.

There _____ so many kids here!

I _____ scared.

But I pretend that I _____ brave.

I walk over to a boy and girl.

"I _____ new here," I say.

"We _____ new here, too!" they say.

Now the three of us _____ friends.

Word Search

Look at the Word Bank.
Circle the words here.
Find each word four times.
Then read the words!

e	j	x	u	a	m	n	a
a	q	a	r	e	k	q	m
r	z	m	f	r	a	k	z
e	n	q	e	a	b	r	e
a	a	r	e	c	z	y	e
c	r	z	a	m	e	x	f

Name _____   Date _____

Look at the Word Bank.
Use the words to fill in the blanks.
Then read the story!

Word Bank

and

together

Nice and Dry

Cat _____ Pup were under an

umbrella _____.

They were nice _____ dry.

Then Bear, Duck, _____ Rabbit came by.

"Come on under," said Cat _____ Pup.

"We can all squeeze _____."

_____ they did!

Word Search

Look at the Word Bank.
Circle the words here.
Find each word four times.
Then read the words!

t	o	g	e	t	h	e	r
a	n	d	q	a	n	d	n
q	a	n	d	a	n	d	d
t	o	g	e	t	h	e	r
t	o	g	e	t	h	e	r
t	o	g	e	t	h	e	r

Sight Words: *any, some*

Look at the Word Bank.
Use the words to fill in the blanks.
Then read the story!

Word Bank

| any |
| some |

Some Beans

Rabbit put _____ lettuce in a bowl.

He added _____ carrots and tomatoes.

"I want to add _____ beans, but I don't

have _____," he said.

Rabbit called Squirrel. "I don't have _____

beans," he said. "Do you?"

Squirrel brought Rabbit _____ beans.

Then they shared a tasty salad.

Word Search

Look at the Word Bank.
Circle the words here.
Find each word four times.
Then read the words!

s	g	x	p	s	a	a	u
j	a	z	a	o	n	u	a
s	q	n	c	m	y	k	n
o	o	u	y	e	a	n	y
m	c	m	s	l	j	q	t
e	j	k	e	s	o	m	e

Sight Words: _be, like_

Look at the Word Bank.
Use the words to fill in the blanks.
Then read the story!

Word Bank

be

like

Will It Be Sunny?

Will the weather _____ hot and sunny?

That would _____ fine with me!

I _____ days that are hot and sunny.

I _____ to go swimming in the lake.

It feels good to _____ in the cool water.

What kind of weather do you _____?

Word Search

Look at the Word Bank.
Circle the words here.
Find each word four times.
Then read the words!

b	d	f	q	l	j	b	g
z	e	b	j	i	i	x	h
p	l	c	r	k	z	k	b
l	i	u	b	e	l	v	e
x	k	l	i	k	e	i	l
b	e	p	q	l	n	z	i

Name _____ Date _____

Look at the Word Bank.
Use the words to fill in the blanks.
Then read the story!

Word Bank

big

small

Big or Small?

An elephant is a _____ animal.

It has a _____ body.

A frog is a _____ animal.

It has a _____ body.

Next to an elephant, I look very _____.

Next to a frog, I look very _____!

Word Search

Look at the Word Bank.
Circle the words here.
Find each word four times.
Then read the words!

e	s	m	a	l	l	q	w
s	x	z	s	b	i	g	b
b	m	s	m	i	v	b	a
i	r	a	a	g	b	c	u
g	x	z	l	k	s	i	j
s	m	a	l	l	q	m	g

Name _____ Date _____

Look at the Word Bank.
Use the words to fill in the blanks.
Then read the story!

Word Bank

can

clean

A Clean House

"Spring is here!" said Mama Bear.

"It's time to _____ our house."

"I _____ scrub," said Papa Bear.

"I _____ mop," said Mama Bear.

"I _____ dust," said Little Bear.

Soon the house was as _____ as _____ be!

"Now let's _____ the yard!" said Little Bear.

Word Search

Look at the Word Bank.
Circle the words here.
Find each word four times.
Then read the words!

c	j	q	c	a	n	p	c
z	a	f	l	l	c	n	l
c	h	n	e	g	e	a	e
a	c	l	a	b	c	a	a
n	x	z	n	q	a	y	n
i	c	l	e	a	n	z	p

Name _____   Date _____

Look at the Word Bank.
Use the words to fill in the blanks.
Then read the story!

Warm Days, Cold Days

Word Bank

cold

warm

On _____ summer days, I try to stay cool.

I swim in a big pool.

I drink ice-_____ lemonade.

On _____ winter days, I try to stay _____.

I wear _____ clothing to play in the

_____ snow.

Word Search

Look at the Word Bank.
Circle the words here.
Find each word four times.
Then read the words!

r	c	o	l	d	u	w	q
w	a	r	m	c	o	a	b
c	c	q	c	w	a	r	m
k	o	t	p	o	a	m	n
b	l	l	w	a	l	r	s
c	d	x	d	g	e	d	m

Name _____   Date _____

Sight Words: *could, find*

Look at the Word Bank.
Use the words to fill in the blanks.
Then read the story!

Word Bank
could
find

How to Find Coco

I _____ not _____ my cat, Coco.

_____ she be hiding in a closet? No.

_____ she be under a bed? No.

Where _____ she be?

Then I had a plan. I put out her favorite food.

I knew Coco would _____ her food.

And then I would _____ Coco!

Look at the Word Bank.
Circle the words here.
Find each word four times.
Then read the words!

f	c	q	c	l	d	x	c
l	i	o	u	n	f	c	o
f	g	n	u	f	i	o	u
f	i	n	d	l	n	u	l
c	o	u	l	d	d	l	d
d	f	z	f	i	n	d	u

Fill-in-the-Blank Stories: Sight Words © 2008 by Linda B. Ross. Scholastic Teaching Resources.

Name _____ Date _____

Look at the Word Bank.
Use the words to fill in the blanks.
Then read the story!

Word Bank

do

don't

Where Do Animals Go?

Where _____ some birds go in winter?

They fly off to warm places.

Most birds _____ like cold weather.

Where _____ squirrels go in winter?

They stay put! Squirrels _____ mind the cold.

Neither _____ rabbits and deer.

Their fur keeps them warm!

Look at the Word Bank.
Circle the words here.
Find each word four times.
Then read the words!

d	f	r	w	d	g	d	o
w	o	'n	d	o	n	't	b
'n	f	n	v	n	m	q	d
d	g	d	't	't	'n	k	o
o	c	j	'n	d	o	j	n
j	u	d	o	l	h	'n	't

Sight Words: *down, up*

Look at the Word Bank.
Use the words to fill in the blanks.
Then read the story!

Word Bank

down

up

Up and Down

The sun comes _____ in the morning.

The rooster crows, "It's time to wake _____!"

A new day has begun.

The sun goes _____ in the evening.

All the animals lay _____ and rest.

They will sleep until the sun comes

_____ again.

Word Search

Look at the Word Bank.
Circle the words here.
Find each word four times.
Then read the words!

d	u	p	d	k	d	f	u
o	q	d	f	o	p	l	h
w	d	j	l	d	w	x	u
n	v	o	h	q	e	n	p
u	l	k	w	d	s	u	h
p	d	o	w	n	u	h	p

Sight Words: *eat, six*

Look at the Word Bank.
Use the words to fill in the blanks.
Then read the story!

Word Bank
eat
six

Let's Eat!

_____ little ants looked for food.

They were hungry and wanted to _____.

They crawled on their _____ little legs.

Finally, they found a crumb to _____.

They split the crumb into _____ tiny pieces.

"Now let's _____ our dinner!" they said.

Word Search

Look at the Word Bank.
Circle the words here.
Find each word four times.
Then read the words!

e	r	e	v	e	s	y	k
d	e	s	a	q	w	i	c
x	a	i	b	t	l	h	x
e	t	x	s	h	s	g	s
a	j	y	d	q	b	i	r
t	s	i	x	e	a	t	x

Sight Words: *fast, run*

Look at the Word Bank.
Use the words to fill in the blanks.
Then read the story!

Word Bank

fast

run

How Fast?

Some animals can _____ very _____.

Cheetahs are as _____ as cars.

Lions and horses are _____ runners, too.

But they can't _____ as _____ as cheetahs.

Other animals aren't _____ at all.

Turtles and snails can't _____ or even

walk _____. They are slow!

Word Search

Look at the Word Bank.
Circle the words here.
Find each word four times.
Then read the words!

b	q	v	f	r	u	d	f
f	a	s	t	r	z	f	a
r	g	f	a	f	u	j	s
r	u	r	k	a	r	n	t
u	c	n	x	s	c	u	q
n	f	a	s	t	k	z	n

Name _____   Date _____

Look at the Word Bank.
Use the words to fill in the blanks.
Then read the story!

Look for Bear

"I can't find Bear," said Squirrel to Rabbit.

"Will you help me _____ _____ him?"

"Yes, let's _____ around," said Rabbit.

They looked _____ a long time.

Then they went to his cave.

"_____! He's sleeping," said Squirrel.

"That means it's time _____ winter."

Word Bank

for

look

Look at the Word Bank.
Circle the words here.
Find each word four times.
Then read the words!

f	q	f	z	l	o	r	l
x	o	o	y	o	z	f	o
l	p	r	l	o	q	o	o
f	o	v	p	k	f	r	k
m	i	o	y	l	o	c	y
l	o	o	k	f	o	r	j

Name _____   Date _____

Look at the Word Bank.
Use the words to fill in the blanks.
Then read the story!

Word Bank

funny

had

A Funny Dream

I _____ a _____ dream.

I was a circus clown!

I _____ a round nose and a _____ hat.

I did _____ things and made people laugh.

I told Mom about the dream I _____.

We both laughed at my _____ dream.

Word Search

Look at the Word Bank.
Circle the words here.
Find each word four times.
Then read the words!

f	h	f	f	d	h	s	m
u	a	z	u	q	f	a	h
n	d	h	y	n	u	v	d
n	e	h	a	d	n	q	h
y	h	a	d	f	n	y	a
e	f	u	n	n	y	w	p

Sight Words: _go, goes_

Look at the Word Bank.
Use the words to fill in the blanks.
Then read the story!

Time to Go!

My sister and I _____ to a great school.

I'm in second grade. She's in first grade.

Our little brother _____ to our school, too.

He's in kindergarten.

We all _____ to school by bus.

Each morning, Mom says, "Let's _____!

The bus is coming!"

Word Bank

go

goes

Look at the Word Bank.
Circle the words here.
Find each word four times.
Then read the words!

s	q	x	a	g	r	j	g
g	g	o	e	s	g	p	o
v	o	l	j	g	z	g	f
g	z	e	g	r	o	o	e
s	g	f	s	x	l	e	j
q	l	o	k	g	o	s	s

Sight Words: *good, my*

Look at the Word Bank.
Use the words to fill in the blanks.
Then read the story!

Word Bank
good
my

A Good Time

Anna is _____ _____ friend.

In fact, she is _____ best friend.

When the weather is _____, we play outside.

When the weather is bad, we play at _____

house or at her house.

We always have a _____ time!

Look at the Word Bank.
Circle the words here.
Find each word four times.
Then read the words!

m	v	k	m	w	g	n	x
g	o	o	d	y	n	m	y
p	g	j	g	o	o	d	f
g	m	o	v	o	m	y	f
x	y	x	o	c	o	j	k
z	e	s	m	d	y	d	a

Name _____ Date _____

Sight Words: *got, were*

Look at the Word Bank.
Use the words to fill in the blanks.
Then read the story!

Word Bank
got
were

We Got Wet!

Bear and his pals _____ having a picnic.

They _____ eating tasty food.

They _____ having a lot of fun.

Then it _____ cloudy.

The sky _____ dark, and it began to rain.

Soon Bear and his pals _____ running home!

Look at the Word Bank.
Circle the words here.
Find each word four times.
Then read the words!

w	d	w	z	g	o	t	p
i	r	e	g	w	e	r	e
w	e	r	e	g	e	v	j
f	g	e	w	k	g	r	y
b	r	o	p	g	o	t	e
x	l	s	t	w	t	p	f

Name _____ Date _____

Look at the Word Bank.
Use the words to fill in the blanks.
Then read the story!

Word Bank

has

have

Who Has a Riddle?

I _____ some riddles to tell you.

What building _____ the most stories?

What are two things you can't _____

for breakfast?

What _____ a ring, but no finger?

Do you _____ any riddles to tell?

Answers: a library; lunch and dinner; a telephone

Look at the Word Bank.
Circle the words here.
Find each word four times.
Then read the words!

h	c	f	h	t	e	h	s
x	a	h	a	j	h	a	v
h	v	v	s	h	a	s	h
l	a	q	e	a	z	f	a
k	o	s	g	v	j	x	v
n	h	a	v	e	j	r	e

Name _____   Date _____

Sight Words: _he, him_

Look at the Word Bank.
Use the words to fill in the blanks.
Then read the story!

Word Bank
he
him

Is He the One?

"Look at _____!" said Rose.

"_____ is so cute!

Can I hold _____?"

The lady at the shelter handed the dog to Rose.

"Is _____ the one you want?" asked Dad.

"Oh, yes!" said Rose. "_____ is the dog for me.

Let's take _____ home."

Word Search

Look at the Word Bank.
Circle the words here.
Find each word four times.
Then read the words!

t	h	h	i	a	e	p	h
b	i	b	h	a	f	o	i
h	m	a	y	p	h	n	m
e	m	h	i	m	e	c	h
k	m	a	v	w	a	y	a
h	e	a	h	i	m	h	e

Fill-in-the-Blank Stories: Sight Words © 2008 by Linda B. Ross. Scholastic Teaching Resources.

37

Name _____   Date _____

Sight Words: *her, she*

Look at the Word Bank.
Use the words to fill in the blanks.
Then read the story!

Word Bank

her

she

Her Special Day

Mimi opened _____ eyes and looked at the clock.

Then _____ jumped out of bed.

_____ brushed _____ teeth and got dressed.

Then _____ ran to the kitchen and

ate _____ breakfast.

Mimi was so excited.

It was _____ first day of school!

Look at the Word Bank.
Circle the words here.
Find each word four times.
Then read the words!

k	s	m	s	v	h	e	r
h	h	l	h	s	g	y	s
d	e	b	z	e	h	h	b
h	v	r	s	h	r	e	s
m	h	g	d	c	g	r	h
x	s	s	h	e	f	p	e

Name _____   Date _____

Look at the Word Bank.
Use the words to fill in the blanks.
Then read the story!

Word Bank

I
me

A Present for Me

Grandpa asked _____ what _____

wanted for my birthday.

_____ said that _____ wanted him to

take _____ to the movies.

_____ also wanted him to buy _____

a big bag of popcorn!

Grandpa said he would do that for _____.

Look at the Word Bank.
Circle the words here.
Find each word four times.
Then read the words!

x	n	m	e	b	q	n	x
f	I	b	c	j	m	I	y
s	m	y	I	q	y	p	m
r	m	f	m	h	d	k	e
m	h	e	c	m	e	y	a
y	s	t	I	f	y	x	r

Name _____ Date _____

Sight Words: *if, then*

Look at the Word Bank.
Use the words to fill in the blanks.
Then read the story!

Word Bank

if

then

If You Move Away

"I'm moving to the city," said Squirrel.

"_____ you move, _____ you'll miss the

tall trees," said Raccoon.

"_____ you move, _____ you'll miss the

fresh air," said Rabbit.

"_____ you move, _____ we'll miss you!"

said Bird.

"Okay," said Squirrel. "_____ I'll stay!"

Word Search

Look at the Word Bank.
Circle the words here.
Find each word four times.
Then read the words!

z	t	s	i	m	q	t	u
i	h	t	f	j	i	h	d
m	f	i	z	t	k	e	t
p	t	h	e	n	h	n	h
t	q	g	t	h	i	e	e
h	i	f	h	n	f	c	n

Name _____ Date _____

Look at the Word Bank.
Use the words to fill in the blanks.
Then read the story!

Word Bank

it

walk

A Long Walk

A ladybug took a _____ on my hand.

_____ was a long _____ for a ladybug!

First, _____ walked on each finger.

Next, _____ took a _____ around my palm.

Then _____ rested before _____ flew away.

Come back soon, little ladybug!

Word Search

Look at the Word Bank.
Circle the words here.
Find each word four times.
Then read the words!

w	p	w	a	l	z	k	i
a	w	b	w	a	i	w	t
e	f	a	h	a	k	a	r
i	a	j	l	y	l	l	g
t	w	a	l	k	n	k	i
w	a	q	i	t	z	r	t

Name _____   Date _____

Sight Words: *jump, our*

Look at the Word Bank.
Use the words to fill in the blanks.
Then read the story!

Word Bank

jump

our

A Big Jump!

_____ cat likes to _____ from high places.

We've seen him _____ from the top of

_____ refrigerator.

He can also _____ from the top of _____

tall bookcase.

_____ dog can't _____ like that!

Word Search

Look at the Word Bank.
Circle the words here.
Find each word four times.
Then read the words!

j	o	u	r	j	u	r	o
j	u	m	n	u	k	o	u
o	g	m	l	m	o	u	j
j	u	q	p	p	u	y	u
o	u	r	y	h	r	l	m
d	q	j	u	m	p	t	p

Fill-in-the-Blank Stories: Sight Words © 2008 by Linda B. Ross. Scholastic Teaching Resources.

Name _____ Date _____

Look at the Word Bank.
Use the words to fill in the blanks.
Then read the story!

Word Bank

kind

know

Now I Know!

"What _____ of animal are you?" asked Calf.

"I'm a duck, and I quack," said Duck.

"I _____ I'm not a duck," said Calf.

"What _____ of animal am I?"

"You're a cow, and you moo," said Duck.

"Now I _____ what I am!" said Calf. "Moo!"

Word Search

Look at the Word Bank.
Circle the words here.
Find each word four times.
Then read the words!

d	j	k	i	n	d	a	k
k	k	n	k	j	f	k	i
n	i	k	m	n	q	n	n
o	l	n	p	v	o	o	d
w	q	o	d	k	z	w	b
k	n	w	k	i	n	d	f

Name _____ Date _____

Look at the Word Bank.
Use the words to fill in the blanks.
Then read the story!

A Long Life

Word Bank

live

long

Some animals _____ a _____ time.

Box turtles can _____ for 100 years!

Alligators can _____ for 50 years.

Other animals don't have a _____ life.

Chipmunks _____ for about three years.

Worker bees _____ for only a few weeks.

What other animal can _____ as

_____ as a box turtle?

Word Search

Look at the Word Bank.
Circle the words here.
Find each word four times.
Then read the words!

l	j	l	u	l	f	t	l
i	e	l	o	n	i	m	i
h	z	i	l	n	a	v	v
l	i	v	e	o	g	r	e
z	a	e	l	o	n	g	p
c	l	o	n	g	e	g	f

Sight Words: _many_, _see_

Look at the Word Bank.
Use the words to fill in the blanks.
Then read the story!

Word Bank

many
see

Many Sights to See

Grandpa and I are in the city.

There are so _____ sights to _____!

We _____ very tall buildings.

We _____ _____ cars and buses.

_____ people are rushing from place to place.

But Grandpa and I take our time.

We want to _____ everything!

Word Search

Look at the Word Bank.
Circle the words here.
Find each word four times.
Then read the words!

m	s	m	i	q	m	s	m
a	r	n	a	j	a	e	a
n	s	m	d	n	n	n	h
y	e	a	c	s	y	v	s
x	e	s	e	z	e	q	e
m	a	n	y	s	e	e	f

Name _____ Date _____

Look at the Word Bank.
Use the words to fill in the blanks.
Then read the story!

Word Bank

new

old

An Old House

"I want a _____ house," said Pig.

"I'm tired of my _____ house."

So Pig looked at many _____ houses.

They looked nice, but they weren't as pretty as

his _____ house.

"I think I'll keep my _____ house," said Pig.

"I'll just buy some _____ things and fix it up!"

Word Search

Look at the Word Bank.
Circle the words here.
Find each word four times.
Then read the words!

s	g	n	p	o	l	n	u
j	n	e	k	l	s	e	g
o	q	e	c	d	n	w	n
l	l	u	w	n	e	q	e
d	c	d	b	l	n	e	w
e	o	l	p	o	l	d	i

Name _____   Date _____

Look at the Word Bank.
Use the words to fill in the blanks.
Then read the story!

Not Now!

Marco went to Jake's house.

"Do you _____ to play?" Marco asked.

"I'm busy _____," said Jake.

Marco asked other friends to play. Everyone was busy!

"Why doesn't anyone _____ to play?" he

thought. "I guess I'll go home _____."

Marco went home. "Surprise!" everyone yelled.

"_____ I understand!" said Marco.

Word Bank
now
want

Look at the Word Bank.
Circle the words here.
Find each word four times.
Then read the words!

n	d	f	n	w	q	w	n
w	o	b	w	z	a	a	h
a	l	w	a	n	t	n	b
n	w	a	v	o	l	t	t
x	r	n	o	w	p	i	l
b	g	t	q	l	n	o	w

Name _____   Date _____

Look at the Word Bank.
Use the words to fill in the blanks.
Then read the story!

Word Bank

| off |
| on |

Lights On, Lights Off

One night, Dad and I were reading.

Suddenly, it got dark! The lights went _____!

Dad turned _____ a flashlight.

Then we looked out the window.

All the lights outside were _____, too.

So Dad and I used a flashlight to read until the lights

came _____ again!

Look at the Word Bank.
Circle the words here.
Find each word four times.
Then read the words!

o	s	m	o	l	w	q	o
l	g	z	s	o	f	f	m
e	o	d	m	f	v	r	o
k	n	f	a	f	b	x	t
f	x	z	f	k	q	o	n
o	n	a	o	f	f	n	i

Name _____ Date _____

Look at the Word Bank.
Use the words to fill in the blanks.
Then read the story!

Word Bank

play

today

Come Out and Play!

"Wake up, Bear!" said Squirrel and Rabbit.

"_____ is the first day of spring.

Come out and _____!"

"We can _____ tag," said Squirrel.

"Let's _____ follow the leader," said Rabbit.

"I just woke up _____," said Bear.

"Let's start with a quiet game!"

Word Search

Look at the Word Bank.
Circle the words here.
Find each word four times.
Then read the words!

c	j	q	t	p	l	a	t
p	p	r	o	o	c	p	o
l	l	l	d	g	d	l	d
a	f	a	a	q	j	a	a
y	p	l	y	y	t	y	y
k	t	o	d	a	y	z	p

Name _____ Date _____

Look at the Word Bank.
Use the words to fill in the blanks.
Then read the story!

Say "Please"

Word Bank

please

say

Once there was a deer that always forgot

to _____ "_____."

One day, she saw a skunk. "Go away!" she said.

"_____ '_____,'" said the skunk.

So the deer said, "_____ go away!"

And the skunk went away!

After that, the deer never forgot to _____

"_____!"

Word Search

Look at the Word Bank.
Circle the words here.
Find each word four times.
Then read the words!

p	c	s	a	y	z	p	q
l	l	a	k	p	o	l	b
s	a	e	s	l	s	e	s
p	l	e	a	s	e	a	a
s	a	v	y	s	l	s	y
p	l	e	a	s	e	e	m

Sight Words: *put, where*

Look at the Word Bank.
Use the words to fill in the blanks.
Then read the story!

Word Bank

put

where

Where Is It?

Marty was a busy monkey.

Sometimes he forgot _____ he

_____ things.

"_____ is my blue cap?" he would ask.

"_____ did I _____ my red socks?"

So Marty _____ labels on his drawers.

Now he knows _____ to _____

things and _____ to find them!

Word Search

Look at the Word Bank.
Circle the words here.
Find each word four times.
Then read the words!

p	w	q	c	p	w	x	p
l	u	h	v	u	h	w	u
p	u	t	e	t	q	h	l
f	w	h	e	r	e	e	p
w	h	u	l	z	e	r	u
p	u	w	h	e	r	e	t

Name _____ Date _____

Look at the Word Bank.
Use the words to fill in the blanks.
Then read the story!

Word Bank

read

when

I Like to Read!

I take out lots of books _____ I go to

the library.

I like to _____ about animals.

_____ I get home, I _____ a book.

It takes me a few weeks to _____ them all.

What do I do _____ I'm finished?

I go back to the library!

Word Search

Look at the Word Bank.
Circle the words here.
Find each word four times.
Then read the words!

w	h	e	p	w	r	e	a
h	w	w	d	h	s	e	r
e	f	h	r	e	a	d	e
n	g	r	e	n	r	e	a
b	r	e	a	n	q	j	d
r	e	a	d	w	h	e	n

Fill-in-the-Blank Stories: Sight Words © 2008 by Linda B. Ross. Scholastic Teaching Resources.

Name _____   Date _____

Look at the Word Bank.
Use the words to fill in the blanks.
Then read the story!

Word Bank
sing
three

Three Plus One

Each morning, _____ birds are

outside my window.

They _____ to me, and I wake up!

Sometimes, I _____ along with them.

When I woke up this morning, guess what I saw?

My _____ little friends, plus one more.

Now four birds will _____ to me!

Look at the Word Bank.
Circle the words here.
Find each word four times.
Then read the words!

t	t	h	r	e	e	f	t
h	h	t	s	i	n	g	h
s	r	s	h	s	w	x	s
i	e	i	c	r	i	n	i
n	e	k	w	x	e	n	n
g	j	t	h	r	e	e	g

Sight Words: *sleep, so*

Look at the Word Bank.
Use the words to fill in the blanks.
Then read the story!

Word Bank

sleep

so

Back to Sleep

Last night I was tired.

_____ I went to _____ early.

My dog, Buddy, went to _____, too.

Suddenly, there was thunder and lightning!

Buddy woke up, and _____ did I.

Buddy was _____ scared, but I wasn't.

I petted him until he went back to _____.

Word Search

Look at the Word Bank.
Circle the words here.
Find each word four times.
Then read the words!

e	s	z	v	s	s	z	k
d	s	l	a	q	l	s	c
s	l	e	e	p	e	l	o
e	e	x	j	e	k	e	a
s	e	y	d	q	p	e	s
o	p	s	o	e	a	p	o

Name _____ Date _____

Look at the Word Bank.
Use the words to fill in the blanks.
Then read the story!

Word Bank

soon

with

Come Back Soon!

Our neighbors went on vacation.

So their parrot is staying _____ us.

Our dog, Jasper, isn't happy _____ our guest.

He started barking as _____ as the bird arrived.

If I spend time _____ the parrot, he gets mad.

Jasper hopes our neighbors come home _____!

Word Search

Look at the Word Bank.
Circle the words here.
Find each word four times.
Then read the words!

b	w	i	l	s	a	k	s
w	i	t	h	w	o	v	o
s	t	s	w	f	i	o	o
w	h	r	o	i	r	t	n
w	i	t	h	o	w	i	h
b	f	s	o	o	n	g	q

Sight Words: *thank, write*

Look at the Word Bank.
Use the words to fill in the blanks.
Then read the story!

Thank You!

Grandma bought me a bike.

I gave her a big hug and said, "_____ you!"

The next day in school, we learned how to

_____ _____-you letters.

So I decided to _____ a letter to Grandma.

Grandma loved my _____-you letter!

Now we _____ letters to each other all the time.

Word Bank
thank
write

Word Search

Look at the Word Bank.
Circle the words here.
Find each word four times.
Then read the words!

w	r	w	r	i	t	e	w
t	r	r	t	x	t	w	r
h	t	i	w	h	h	r	i
a	h	t	t	v	a	i	t
n	l	e	s	e	n	n	e
k	t	h	a	n	k	q	k

 Fill-in-the-Blank Stories: Sight Words © 2008 by Linda B. Ross. Scholastic Teaching Resources.

Name _____ Date _____

Look at the Word Bank.
Use the words to fill in the blanks.
Then read the story!

Word Bank

the

them

The Best Cats

I have _____ best cats!

I named one of _____ Abby, and

_____ other one Tabby.

Each day, I feed _____ and give

_____ water.

Which one do I like _____ best?

I love _____ both the same!

Word Search

Look at the Word Bank.
Circle the words here.
Find each word four times.
Then read the words!

e	t	f	c	t	h	s	t
t	h	e	m	h	f	k	h
h	d	y	s	t	r	t	e
e	l	t	h	e	h	h	m
q	t	h	d	f	n	e	v
t	h	e	t	h	g	m	m

Sight Words: *their, they*

Look at the Word Bank.
Use the words to fill in the blanks.
Then read the story!

Word Bank

their
they

Can They Jump?

Frogs live in two places.

_____ live on land and in the water.

_____ strong hind legs help them jump

from place to place.

What do frogs eat? _____ like to eat insects.

_____ use _____ long, sticky

tongues to catch them!

Look at the Word Bank.
Circle the words here.
Find each word four times.
Then read the words!

s	t	t	h	e	y	t	h
t	t	h	e	i	r	h	t
h	h	t	e	g	t	e	h
v	e	e	h	y	h	i	g
s	i	q	i	e	e	r	j
t	r	t	h	r	y	n	y

Name _____   Date _____

Look at the Word Bank.
Use the words to fill in the blanks.
Then read the story!

Fun for Us!

Aunt Josie took _____ to a petting zoo.

_____ were many animals to pet.

_____ were rabbits and turtles.

_____ were also horses, cows, and sheep.

The zookeeper even let _____ pet a

snake while she held it!

It took _____ all day to pet all the animals!

Word Bank

there

us

Look at the Word Bank.
Circle the words here.
Find each word four times.
Then read the words!

t	t	k	u	z	t	u	s
t	h	e	r	e	h	s	v
p	h	r	t	h	e	r	e
g	u	e	v	o	r	m	u
x	s	x	r	c	e	u	n
t	h	r	u	e	y	f	s

Name _____   Date _____

Look at the Word Bank.
Use the words to fill in the blanks.
Then read the story!

Word Bank
too
two

Two Lost Chicks

_____ little chicks took a walk.

They wandered off _____ far and got lost.

"I'm scared," said one chick.

"I'm scared, _____," said the other.

They started to cry, and Mama Hen heard them.

"Where have you _____ been?" she asked.

"I missed you!"

"We missed you, _____!" said the chicks.

Word Search

Look at the Word Bank.
Circle the words here.
Find each word four times.
Then read the words!

t	w	t	w	o	j	q	p
u	k	w	g	t	w	o	l
t	o	o	z	x	o	t	j
t	w	m	t	w	u	o	t
b	j	o	w	o	q	o	w
x	t	s	b	u	o	p	f

Sight Words: *was, what*

Look at the Word Bank.
Use the words to fill in the blanks.
Then read the story!

Word Bank

was

what

What a Mess!

Percy's sink _____ leaking.

"_____ should I do?" he asked.

There _____ water everywhere!

"I'll call Pilar," he said.

"She'll know _____ to do."

Pilar _____ there in a flash.

Soon the sink _____ as good as new!

Word Search

Look at the Word Bank.
Circle the words here.
Find each word four times.
Then read the words!

w	c	f	w	h	a	w	s
x	h	w	a	j	w	a	v
w	v	a	s	w	a	s	w
l	a	q	t	h	z	f	h
w	o	s	g	a	w	x	a
n	w	h	a	t	j	r	t

Sight Words: *we, went*

Look at the Word Bank.
Use the words to fill in the blanks.
Then read the story!

Word Bank

we
went

Up We Went!

_____ took a ride on a Ferris wheel.

_____ _____ all the way up.

Then _____ stopped at the top!

_____ could see everything in the park.

Then _____ came all the way down.

_____ _____ around and around

ten times. I know, because I counted!

Word Search

Look at the Word Bank.
Circle the words here.
Find each word four times.
Then read the words!

a	q	v	v	r	u	d	w
b	w	e	n	t	z	w	e
w	g	f	t	f	u	e	k
s	e	p	k	w	e	n	t
g	d	n	h	s	c	t	w
n	f	e	t	w	e	z	e

Name _____   Date _____

Look at the Word Bank.
Use the words to fill in the blanks.
Then read the story!

Word Bank
who
will

Friends Will Help

"_____ _____ help me fix up

my yard?" asked Rabbit.

"I _____ cut the grass," said Bear.

"I _____ plant flowers," said Chipmunk.

"We _____ pull weeds," said the squirrels.

Rabbit and his friends worked hard all day.

"Now I _____ cook dinner for you,"

said Rabbit. "_____ is hungry?"

Word Search

Look at the Word Bank.
Circle the words here.
Find each word four times.
Then read the words!

k	w	i	l	l	w	c	w
w	h	o	b	w	w	h	v
i	o	q	w	i	i	h	o
l	v	r	w	h	r	l	s
l	w	i	y	c	o	r	l
w	h	w	i	l	l	d	e

Name _____ Date _____

Look at the Word Bank.
Use the words to fill in the blanks.
Then read the story!

Word Bank
you
your

What Did You Forget?

Leo is going out to play ball.

"Do _____ have _____ cap?" asked Mom.

Leo ran to get his cap.

"What about _____ bat and _____ mitt?"

asked Mom. Leo ran to get them.

"What else did you forget?" asked Mom.

"I forgot to give _____ a hug!" said Leo.

Word Search

Look at the Word Bank.
Circle the words here.
Find each word four times.
Then read the words!

y	o	u	y	o	u	r	y
l	x	p	z	o	y	f	o
y	y	w	y	l	u	t	j
y	o	j	o	s	y	r	y
o	q	u	u	y	f	m	o
u	k	l	r	b	y	o	u

   Fill-in-the-Blank Stories: Sight Words © 2008 by Linda B. Ross. Scholastic Teaching Resources.